Serum Making Class

Serum Making Class:
Facial Serums, Aloe Vera Gel, Hand Sanitizer, Gel Eye Shadow, Gel Eyeliner, and Mascara

Soapmaking Studio Class Workbook

Student Edition

Kerri Mixon

Acute Publications
Spring Valley

Kerri Mixon is a 16th generation soapmaker and the owner of multiple soap-related businesses. Her articles on making soap and cosmetics have appeared in numerous trade publications. A seasoned instructor, she has taught classes to students and live audiences across the United States. Master soapmaker Kerri Mixon's passion for making soap and cosmetics is obviously contagious; several graduates of her classes now run their own successful soap, body care, and cosmetics businesses.

More Soapmaking Studio Class Workbooks by Kerri Mixon

Serum Making Class: Facial Serums, Aloe Vera Gel, Hand Sanitizer, Gel Eye Shadow, Gel Eyeliner, and Mascara
Soapmaking Studio Class Workbook
By Kerri Mixon

Acute Publications, Spring Valley 91976
© 2016 by Kerri Mixon
Printed in the United States of America.

ISBN-13: 978-0692705124
ISBN-10: 0692705120

Dedication

This book is dedicated to the Handcrafted Soap and Cosmetic Guild, the professional trade organization that acknowledged the important value of teaching home crafters to make products from water based serums.

It is also dedicated to the readers and home crafters who will enjoy creating effective serum treatments for themselves and others.

What's a Serum? (And Do You Need One?)
By Courtney Dunlop

As you're shopping for skin care products and reading endless articles about the latest and greatest skin savers, you've probably come across loads of products called serums.

But...what exactly is a serum? And more important, should you use one?

Cosmetic chemists and dermatologists maintain serums tend to be more effective than plain ol' moisturizers due to the method of delivery: Serums are more concentrated with active ingredients, so they're able to penetrate more deeply than creams. That makes these products ideal for troubleshooting specific problems such as redness, acne, and hyperpigmentation. For example, rosacea sufferers might try a serum that contains azulene, which can help calm irritated skin.

They're also ideal for oily-skinned folks who avoid heavy creams like the plague. Most serums are water-based (therefore non-pore-clogging), making them ideal for shiny-prone skin.

For normal or dry skin, serums can be layered under cream for a one-two punch. For instance, vitamin C serums are known far and wide for brightening brown spots and giving skin a youthful glow, but vitamin C is rarely found concentrated enough in a cream to make much difference.

Of course, concentrated ingredients also mean a steeper price tag, but since you only use two to three drops at a time (any more than that will make you sticky), one bottle lasts a long time, which takes some of the bite out of the cost.

So, back to the original question: Do you need a serum? I say if you have found your current skin care regimen has plateaued and you'd like to jumpstart your complexion, it's definitely worth giving one a try.

Courtney Dunlop, "What's a Serum? (And Do You Need One?)," *Doctor Oz* (blog), January 28, 2013 (1:15 p.m.), http://blog.doctoroz.com /oz-experts/whats-a-serum-and-do-you-need-one.

Contents

Preface

In my late teens and early twenties, I suffered from occasional outbreaks of facial acne. Not only was the experience painful, it was also socially devastating. At the time, the common over-the-counter treatments always included benzoyl peroxide creams and salicylic acid washes. The treatments were so harsh they left my facial skin dry, hard, cracked, red, and tender. Now, with more worldly experiences under my belt, when I think back to the drug store acne treatments, I'd compare the texture of my post-treatment skin to dermal tissue having a mild chemical burn.

Out of desperation, I finally went to a dermatologist who explained the harsh ingredients to me. First, he explained topical benzoyl peroxide was a bactericide, meaning it chemically killed the bacteria present on the outer layer of skin that commonly caused acne. The salicylic acid "burned away" or dissolved dead skin cells that may have otherwise remained on the surface to clog pores. So, likening the after-effect of the harsh treatments to a mild chemical burn seems fairly accurate.

Second, the dermatologist explained the comedogenicity scale and how specific skin care ingredients have been ranked as to their likelihood to clog skin pores. After researching ingredients as he suggested, I noticed most any ingredient that was oil based, oil derived, or oil soluble had a significantly higher likeliness of clogging pores.

Third, he explained active skin care ingredients are delivered more efficiently to deeper layers of skin tissue when they are in a water based serum or gel. Oil tends to clog pores because it rests as a heavy coating atop the outer layer of dermis, unable to be truly absorbed by the skin. Water has the ability to pass through skin cells through osmosis and penetrate to deeper layers of skin. The active ingredients dissolved in the water also penetrate to a deeper layer through diffusion.

After my eye opening experience with the dermatologist and subsequent research, I learned to request acne "serums" because the serums were always water based. Even in the 1990s I found serums at the cosmetic counters in department stores, such as Buffum's, Bullock's, Macy's, May Co, and Nordstrom. Later I found more natural versions lacking the robust preservatives at the cosmetic counters in Whole Foods and other health food stores.

As the curriculum for formulating cosmetics at the Soapmaking Studio advanced and the Serum Making Class became more popular, I searched Google and YouTube to review what sorts of serums others were making at home. I was rather alarmed to learn most instructions and videos available on the Internet consisted of essential oils added to base/carrier oils. In other words, they detailed the creation of a product parallel to a scented massage oil but erroneously entitled it a "serum." I could only imagine a person in need of a water based product, miserably trying to successfully use a vial of olive oil containing a few drops of essential oil.

At that time, karma saw fit for me to give a presentation on the formulation of water based serums to the hundreds of attendees of the Handcrafted Soap and Cosmetic Guild in Tampa, Florida. To supplement my presentation, I thought it would be nice to unveil a book on making serums, so I began transposing the Soapmaking Studio workbook on making serums into a published book.

Acknowledgments

The Skin Deep ingredient scores were obtained from the Environmental Workgroup's online Skin Deep database at http://www.ewg.org/skindeep/. Although ingredient scores change over time, all are current as of the publication date of this book.

If it were not for the involvement of the Handcrafted Soap and Cosmetic Guild requesting author Kerri Mixon give a presentation on the formulation of serums, this book would not have been published.

Introduction

Although originally intended as the class workbook for the Serum Making Class at the Soapmaking Studio in Lemon Grove, California, this book may serve as a standalone instruction manual for making serums if the reader is already familiar with good manufacturing practices for home crafters, weighing ingredients accurately on a scale, and home cosmetics crafting in general.

This book includes a recipe and instructions for making a concentrated serum base. It is intended the serum base will be made into a finished product, such as a facial serum, aloe vera gel, gel eye shadow, or gel eyeliner. A section of this book includes recipes and instructions for making the serum base into such products through the addition of specific active ingredients. This book also includes a section detailing the different active ingredients, their Skin Deep database scores, common uses, appropriate quantities, constraint parameters, and perceived benefits.

Chapter 1
Good Manufacturing Practices

Good manufacturing practices ensure a safe and consistently reliable cosmetic product is produced from each batch prepared. Good manufacturing practices progress from ingredient documentation, to stock rotation and storage logs, to standard operating procedures. Good manufacturing practices include accurate recordkeeping and the ability to track ingredients and source suppliers for each batch of product made. Through accurate recordkeeping, the handcrafter is able to guarantee product integrity. Standard operating procedures assist employees in preparing the same product each time it is made, without varying factors, such as times and temperatures, that may alter the product's thickness, color, or scent. Good manufacturing practices also include preventing product contamination from all three contamination sources:

1. Biological contaminants (ants, flies, plants, fungi, bacteria, and etc.)
2. Chemical contaminants (soap residue inside a container, pesticide residue from a flea "bomb," a drop of oil intended for a squeaky hinge, a drop of butane while filling a lighter, and etc.)
3. Physical contaminants (paperclip, piece of glass, dust, cat hair, human hair, and etc.)

Marie Gale

For more detailed information on how to run a truly professional cosmetics manufacturing business incorporating good manufacturing practices, refer to the book <u>Good Manufacturing Practices for Soap & Cosmetic Handcrafters</u> by Marie Gale, available from http://astore.amazon.com/soapstudio-20/detail/0979594545 with ISBN-10: 0979594545 or ISBN-13: 978-0979594540 and first published by Cinnabar Press in 2013.

Chapter 2
About Serum

What is a serum? Serums are extremely concentrated and potent skincare cosmetics. Serums are always water based and designed to be easily absorbed by the skin. Serums sink in and penetrated much deeper than products containing oil, which only rest atop the outer dermis layer. Depending on the exact additives, most serums are designed to be gentler than lotions or creams because there are no oils to irritate sensitive or acneic skin types. Because serums are absorbed completely by the skin, they are sheer and weightless underneath a lotion, cream, or sunblock.

So, for example, a vitamin C serum delivers a more intensive dose of vitamin C to deeper layers of skin. It may be used alone by someone suffering from acne, who is avoiding excessive oils. It may be used by someone with sensitive skin underneath protective sunblock. It may also be used by someone with aging skin and applied before a daily moisturizer or thick night cream.

The water based gel body of a commercial serum is often thickened with carbomer (as in commercial aloe vera gel) or other acrylates. Carbomer and other acrylates are derived from inorganic petrochemicals that thicken with increased pH (above pH 6). Effective skin care products frequently target a final product pH between pH 4 and pH 5. Carbomers generally require too high of a pH for skin applications. With today's natural ingredient surge, customers who understand the inorganic sourcing of carbomer tend to avoid products containing it.

While guar gum and xanthan gum are natural ingredients that will form a clear gel, they are unstable because their polysaccharides are attracted to neighboring polysaccharides with a greater affinity than to the water. Therefore, the natural gums tend to be very stringy, have a finish similar to mucous, and permanently trap air bubbles within the gel. The natural gums may also incur an irreversible "fish eye" stage. Also, the gums are anionic (negatively charge) and will neutralize the cationic (positively charged) active ingredients.

The most natural, sheer, water based serums are made with hydroxyethyl cellulose, which is a natural wood cellulose. Hydroxyethyl cellulose is nonionic, meaning it is completely neutral and will not interfere with the active ingredients. It absorbs water with tremendous consistency and evenness. The gel is not stringy and "fish eyes" may be corrected with mechanical mixing. Unlike carbomer and other acrylates, it can be more difficult to use in a formulation because it requires patience to allow the HEC to fully hydrate. The added benefit of hydroxyethyl cellulose is the thin, breathable barrier remaining on the skin; it helps to seal and protect skin, thus its common use in protective scar prevention serums.

Although fairly easy to make, crafters who manufacture serums for resale must remember two important aspects of serum creation: 1. Even though the main ingredient is water, serums are generally more expensive and sell for more than lotions because serums are more effective and contain expensive beneficial additives in high concentrations. 2. Water based products increase the potential for microbial growth and must include trustworthy preservatives to prevent biological contamination.

Chapter 3
Choosing Additives

When formulating serums, it is important to remember serums are water based; therefore, all additives should be water based. If including an oil phase and an emulsifier, the crafter is making a lotion, not a serum.

Water phase additives take careful consideration, mostly determined by the constraints of the preservative. For example, some preservatives may be denatured or deactivated by a specific pH range or by increased temperature. Some additives are very sensitive to product pH, such as niacinamide's (vitamin B3's) chemical conversion to nicotinic acid through hydrolysis, in either products that are too acidic or too alkaline. Therefore, some serum products must undergo a pH adjustment or be "pH balanced" to accommodate specific additives. Some additives, such as liposomes, incorporate a semi-water soluble ingredient encapsulated in a microscopic water disbursable phospholipid package. Although extremely stable under normal conditions, some liposomes are damaged by either heat or mechanical mixing above 500 rpm and must be added when the product is cool and must be mixed in by stirring by hand. Creating a serum is truly like working a puzzle and verifying all active ingredients can exist harmoniously in the same serum.

So, when choosing additives, consider the following:
1. Will the additive be damaged or altered by the pH of the product?
2. Will the pH of the additive adjust the final pH of the product to denature the preservative or render the preservative ineffective?
3. Can the additive be damaged by heat? Must the additive be incorporated after the product has cooled?
4. Will the additive be destroyed by mechanical mixing? If so, can it be mixed in by hand after the other additives are blended into the product?
5. Does the additive have and off or unpleasant odor? Will the additive still be effective or still have an unpleasant odor if used in a smaller percentage?

One of the most difficult choices when making serums is considering preservatives. Each preservative has different parameters for use. For example, a few constraints for some preservatives:
1. Aspen Bark Extract (destroyed by high heat and extreme pH).
2. Germaben II (destroyed by high heat or extreme pH).
3. Germall Plus (destroyed by high heat or extreme pH).
4. GSB (Gluconolactone & Sodium Benzoate) (destroyed by extreme pH).
5. Optiphen Plus (destroyed by high heat or high pH).
6. PhytoCide (not water soluble, destroyed by high pH).
7. Potassium Sorbate (not effective against bacteria, destroyed by high pH).
8. VegeCide (only for anhydrous products).

When considering the social acceptance of an ingredient, this book refers to the Environmental Workgroup's Skin Deep online database of cosmetic ingredients. Lower scores (1-6) are generally better and higher scores (7-10) are less desirable. An ingredient with a score of 2 with limited data availability may improve to a score of 1 or may worsen to a score of 3 as more data becomes available. A score of 0 usually indicates no data is available on the ingredient. Data availability may range from "none," to "limited," to "fair," to "good," to "robust."

Chapter 4
Additives and Ingredients

Allantoin
INCI: *Allantoin*
Purpose: Skin healing, regeneration, and conditioning.
Skin Deep Database Score: 1
Skin Deep Data Available: Fair
Source: Plant (organic) or synthetic

Allantoin, derived from the root of the comfrey plant, is a trusted conditioning additive for skin healing preparations. After-injury, post-tattoo, stretch mark, and scar recovery products always contain allantoin. White dry powder. Add to water phase from 0.5% to 2.0% of the total weight of the product. First, add to room temperature water, then heat solution to 130° F to ensure solvation.

Aloe Vera (200X)
INCI: *Aloe vera (Aloe barbadensis) leaf juice extract*
Purpose: Skin conditioning, renewal, and healing.
Skin Deep Database Score: 1
Skin Deep Data Available: Limited
Source: Plant (organic)

Aloe vera powder is the inner gel portion of the aloe vera leaf that has been juiced, freeze-dried, and powdered. 200X is the organic, 200 times concentrated version. It contains polysaccharides, vitamins (E, A, D, and B12), enzymes (including bradykinase that is known to break down dead skin cells to help keep wounds clean and promote new cell growth), anthraquinones (such as aloin and emodin that act as natural pain killers), amino acids, and salicylic acid (a natural anti-inflammatory with anti-bacterial properties). White dry powder. Store dry powder in a dark container, away from light because aloe vera juice powder is damaged by UV light. For true reconstituted aloe vera juice, add 1 part aloe vera (200X) powder to 199 parts water. Add to water phase from 0.2% to 0.5% of the total weight of the product. May impart an undesirable grassy odor to products. Reconstituted juice is beige to pale yellow in color. Complete dissolution may take up to 20 minutes.

Organic aloe vera juice powder, 200 times concentrated.

Aspen Bark Extract
INCI: *Aspen (Populus tremuloides) bark extract*
Purpose: Skin renewal, lightening, and pore refinement. Product anti-bacterial preservative.
Skin Deep Database Score: 1
Skin Deep Data Available: Limited
Source: Plant (organic)

Aspen bark extract is a valuable double duty additive. It is an effective natural preservative if specific criteria are met. As a preservative, it must not be heated above 140° F and the final product must have a pH ranging from pH 3.0 to pH 9.0, or else the anti-microbial properties are rendered ineffective. Aspen bark extract is also a natural source of salicylates (specifically, salicylic acid), which are used as analgesics and for pore refinement and acne control. Salicylic acid (a natural beta hydroxy acid) represents from 54% to 60% of the aspen bark extract. White dry powder. Aspen bark extract is UV light sensitive and should be stored in darkness or inside UV inhibiting material. This additive is acidic and may lower the pH of the products to which it is added. Add to water phase from 1.5% to 3.5% of the total weight of the product, which must have a final pH between 3.0 and 9.0; do not heat above 140° F. High temperature or extreme pH will damage this preservative.

Cetearyl Alcohol 30/70 or **Cetearyl Alcohol 70/30**
INCI: *Cetearyl alcohol*
Purpose: Product emulsifier, thickener, viscosity stabilizer.
Skin Deep Database Score: 1
Skin Deep Data Available: Limited
Source: Plant (organic) or synthetic

A powerful emulsifier and humectant used in lotions and creams, cetearyl alcohol is a mixture of naturally derived fatty alcohols consisting of cetyl alcohol (C16, from coconut oil) and stearyl alcohol (C18, from stearic acid). The 30/70 is 30% cetyl alcohol and 70% stearyl alcohol; it melts at 130° F and forms a thicker, stiffer emulsion. The 70/30 is 70% cetyl alcohol and 30% stearyl alcohol; it melts at 124° F and forms a looser, softer emulsion. The cetearyl alcohol 30/70 contains less cetyl alcohol and is non-irritating to people with eczema. Both are in the form of white waxy flakes (pastilles). Usually added to oil phase from 1% to 3% of the total weight of the product. Using more in lotions and creams will cause "soaping" (the appearance of white streaks on the skin). Use up to 10% in mascara products where the cetearyl alcohol is the only thickener (no stearic acid) or for a stiffer product.

Cyclomethicone
INCI: *Cyclomethicone*
Purpose: Hair, skin, and lash conditioning, anti-static, emollient, humectant. Product thinning.
Skin Deep Database Score: 2
Skin Deep Data Available: Limited
Source: Mineral (inorganic)

This natural oil-soluble liquid thins the viscosity of mascara so in may be applied to the lashes, then it quickly evaporates cleanly away. Unlike alcohol, it does not feel cool as it evaporates. The added benefit of cyclomethicone is that it acts as an anti-static lubricant to separate lashes and as a conditioner. Because it is oil soluble, it requires the addition of an emulsifier. Clear fluid liquid. Odorless. Add to oil phase from 1% to 15% of the total weight of the product.

Germaben II

INCI: *Propylene glycol, diazolidinyl urea, methylparaben, and propylparaben*
Purpose: Product broad spectrum preservative.
Skin Deep and information per ingredient:

	Propylene glycol	Diazolidinyl urea	Methylparaben	Propylparaben
Database Scores	3	6	4	7
Data Available	Fair	Limited	Limited	Limited
Source	Mineral (inorganic) or synthetic	Animal (organic) or synthetic	Mineral (inorganic) or synthetic	Mineral (inorganic) or synthetic

This water-soluble liquid preservative is effective against Gram-positive bacteria, Gram-negative bacteria, yeast, and mold. Not for use in lip products. Clear fluid liquid. Add to water phase from 0.5% to 1.0% of the total weight of the product. High temperature will damage this ingredient: After being added, the product must not be heated above 140° F. Final product pH must remain between pH 3.0 and 7.5.

Germall Plus

INCI: *Propylene glycol, diazolidinyl urea, and iodopropynyl butylcarbamate*
Purpose: Product broad spectrum preservative.
Skin Deep and information per ingredient:

	Propylene glycol	Diazolidinyl urea	Iodopropynyl butylcarbamate
Database Scores	3	6	5
Data Available	Fair	Limited	Limited
Source	Mineral (inorganic) or synthetic	Animal (organic) or synthetic	Mineral (inorganic) or synthetic

This paraben-free water-soluble liquid preservative is effective against Gram-positive bacteria, Gram-negative bacteria, yeast, mold, and spores. Excels in high-pigment products, such as gel eye shadow and mascara. Not for use in lip products. Not for use in sprays or aerosols. Clear fluid liquid. Add to water phase from 0.1% to 0.5% of the total weight of the product. High temperature will damage this ingredient: After being added, the product must not be heated above 122° F. Final product pH must be between pH 3.0 and 8.0.

Glycerin

INCI: *Glycerin*
Synonyms: Glycerol, Glycyl alcohol.
Purpose: Skin humectant, conditioning, emollient.
Skin Deep Database Score: 2
Skin Deep Data Available: Good
Source: Plant (organic)

Chemically, glycerin is a sugar alcohol. Historically, glycerin was animal sourced, which is uncommon today. Vegetable glycerin is a clear odorless humectant used to retain skin moisture. Too much glycerin will make a serum seem sticky and heavy. (Also see "propanediol," which is very similar but thinner and less sticky.) A clear viscous liquid. Odorless. Add to water phase of products from 1% to 10% of the total weight of the product.

GSB

INCI: *Gluconolactone and sodium benzoate*
Purpose: Product anti-bacterial and anti-fungal preservative.
Skin Deep and information per ingredient:

	Gluconodeltalactone	Sodium benzoate
Database Scores	1	6
Data Available	Limited	Limited
Source	Animal (organic)	Mineral (inorganic) or synthetic

A truly water-soluble natural preservative that is EcoCert certified and generally regarded as safe and provides effective broad spectrum preservation. Not for use in products containing ascorbic acid or certain food colors due to conversion of sodium benzoate to benzoic acid and in the presence of heat, metal ions and ultraviolet light, possible conversion to benzene. A white powder that may be added at any time to the water phase. Use from 0.75% to 2.0%. Final product must maintain a pH between pH 3.0 and 6.0.

Honeyquat

INCI: *Hydroxypropyltrimonium honey*
Purpose: Skin and hair conditioning, humectant, emollient, anti-static.
Skin Deep Database Score: 1
Skin Deep Data Available: None
Source: Mineral (inorganic) but not vegan due to bee labor

Honeyquat is a naturally derived quaternized conditioning agent made from honey and has excellent moisture binding capabilities (far more powerful than glycerin). The hydroxy groups of the disaccharides are modified and a quaternary cationic polymer is formed. The positive charge of honeyquat allows it to bind to negatively-charged damaged areas of hair and skin to offer moisturizing and conditioning. Honeyquat also reduces static electricity in hair. It is a natural antioxidant, an anti-inflammatory, is high in vitamin C, and promotes collagen formation in the skin. It is an excellent cleansing agent while improving skin texture and surface smoothness. Thin yellow liquid with a mild characteristically fishy odor. Add to water phase from 1% to 3% of the total weight of the product. If able to detect a fishy odor, add an odor neutralizing fragrance oil mixed with an equal amount of polysorbate 20 or 80 so the fragrance will stay mixed into the water phase.

Hydroxyethyl Cellulose

INCI: *Hydroxyethyl cellulose*
Synonyms: 2-hydroxyethyl cellulose, Cellulose, HEC, HE cellulose.
Purpose: Skin protecting. Product thickener, gel forming. Viscosity stabilizer.
Skin Deep Database Score: 1
Skin Deep Data Available: Fair
Source: Plant (organic) or synthetic

Used as a gelling agent, a thickener, and an emulsion stabilizer. Hydroxyethyl cellulose is a non-ionic rheology modifier derived from wood cellulose that changes the flow properties of water. Continued on next page.

Hydroxyethyl cellulose continued from previous page.
Serums are designed to contain high concentrations of beneficial active ingredients dissolved in water; water is too thin to be applied topically and the active ingredients prevent application through a spray. The logical choice is to create a gel to thicken the water for easy application. HEC is a natural ingredient, rich with beneficial polysaccharides, and makes the perfect serum base. Dry white powder. Add to water phase before other ingredients from 0.5% to 2.0% of the total weight of the product. Stir or mix mechanically for the first 20 minutes to ensure even hydration in distilled water. Heating the mixture will increase the rate of hydration slightly. If uneven gelling occurs from a lack of stirring, mechanical mixing will create an even gel consistency. The resulting gel will be mostly clear, not crystal clear, and should be preserved. Some preservatives will give the gel a milky appearance.

Dry hydroxyethyl cellulose powder.

Liposome C
INCI: *Water, Glycerin, phospholipid, and sodium ascorbyl phosphate*
Purpose: Skin nutrient, antioxidant, collagen production, deep delivery vitamin C.
Skin Deep and information per ingredient:

	Water	Glycerin	Phospholipid	Sodium ascorbyl phosphate
Database Scores	1	2	1	1
Data Available	Robust	Good	Fair	Limited
Source	Mineral (inorganic)	Plant (organic)	Plant (organic)	Mineral (inorganic) or synthetic

Liposome C (liposomal encapsulated vitamin C) is sodium ascorbyl phosphate in a liposomal delivery system. Liposomal delivery systems are microscopic vesicles consisting of an aqueous center and a phospholipid outer membrane. Vitamin C is commonly added to products to encourage collagen production within the skin, to lighten skin discoloration and dark spots, and to reverse sun damage because it inhibits melanin production. Dark yellow fluid liquid. Add to water phase from 2.00% to 10.00% of the total weight of the product. This acidic fluid may reduce the pH of the product. High temperature or high mixing speeds will damage this ingredient: After being added, the product must not be heated above 110° F and must not be mixed faster than 500 rpm (so only mix by hand).

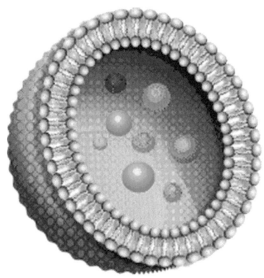
Liposome

Liposome CoQ10
INCI: *Water, phospholipid, and ubiquinone*
Purpose: Skin nutrient, collagen production, deep delivery CoQ10.
Skin Deep and information per ingredient:

	Water	Glycerin	Ubiquinone
Database Scores	1	2	1
Data Available	Robust	Good	Fair
Source	Mineral (inorganic)	Plant (organic)	Plant (organic)

Liposome CoQ10 (liposomal encapsulated co-enzyme Q10) is ubiquinone in a liposomal delivery system. Liposomal delivery systems are microscopic vesicles consisting of an aqueous center and a phospholipid outer membrane. This co-enzyme Q10 is an extremely powerful water-soluble antioxidant. It boots skin repair and skin regeneration, reduces damage by free radicals (such as brown age spots and wrinkles), and the small particle size penetrates skin cells easily for efficient delivery deep into skin tissue. Orange fluid liquid. Add to water phase from 2.00% to 10.00% of the total weight of the product. High temperature or high mixing speeds will damage this ingredient: After being added, the product must not be heated above 110° F and must not be mixed faster than 500 rpm (so only mix by hand).

Mineral Pigment
INCI: *Iron oxide or ultramarine or chromium oxide*
Purpose: Mascara, eyeliner, and/or eye shadow colorant.
Skin Deep and information per ingredient:

	Iron oxide	Ultramarine	Chromium oxide
Color	Black or brown	Blue or purple	Green or teal
Database Scores	2	3	3
Data Available	Fair	Limited	Limited
Source	Mineral (inorganic) or synthetic	Mineral (inorganic) or synthetic	Mineral (inorganic) or synthetic

Mineral Pigment continued from previous page.

The term "mineral pigment" may refer to an iron oxide (black or brown), an ultramarine (blue or purple), or chromium oxide (green). Iron oxide is synthetic mineral pigment recognized by the FDA in 1977 as safe for use in "cosmetics generally, including eye area use" and iron oxides are considered the safest, stable colorant available. Both ultramarine (in 1976) and chromium oxide (in 1977) are synthetic mineral pigments recognized by the FDA as safe for use in "externally applied cosmetics, including eye area use." Unlike activated charcoal, mineral pigments may be safely used to color eye liner and mascara. Mineral pigments may be combined to create additional colors, such as "blue black."

Niacinamide
INCI: *Niacinamide*
Synonym: Vitamin B3.
Purpose: Skin nutrient, lightener, tightener, collagen production.
Skin Deep Database Score: 1
Skin Deep Data Available: Fair
Source: Plant (organic) or synthetic

Niacinamide, the active form of vitamin B3, is necessary for cellular energy and optimal tissue function. It reduces fine lines, wrinkles, aids in natural exfoliation, assists the skin renovation process, and improves hydration through natural moisture retention. Niacinamide is used in commercial preparations for treating loose sagging skin, oily or acneic skin, rough patchy skin, sun damaged skin, and uneven skin tone. It is found in almost every anti-aging skincare product. Dry white powder. At 2% it effectively boosts collagen synthesis; at 4% it effectively treats oily and acneic skin; at 5% it reduces age spots and uneven skin tone. Add to water phase of products from 2% to 5% of the total weight of the product, which must have a final pH between 3.0 and 7.5. Extreme pH will damage this ingredient and convert it into nicotinic acid (niacin), a less usable form of vitamin B3.

Optiphen Plus
INCI: *Phenoxyethanol, caprylyl glycol, and sorbic acid*
Purpose: Product broad spectrum preservative.
Skin Deep and information per ingredient:

	Phenoxyethanol	*Caprylyl glycol*	*Sorbic acid*
Database Scores	4	1	3
Data Available	Limited	Limited	Fair
Source	Mineral (inorganic) or synthetic	Plant (organic)	Plant (organic)

This paraben-free water-soluble liquid preservative is effective against Gram-positive bacteria, Gram-negative bacteria, yeast, and mold. Perfect for use in acidic products. Not for use in lip products. May solidify (harden) below 77° F; if solidification occurs due to low temperatures, simply warm Optiphen Plus container to 95° F and shake or mix thoroughly. Pale yellow fluid liquid. Add to water phase from 0.75% to 1.5% of the total weight of the product, which must have a final pH below 6.0; do not heat above 176° F. High temperature or high pH will damage this preservative.

Panthenol
INCI: *Panthenol*
Synonyms: Pantethoic acid, ProVitamin B5.
Purpose: Skin conditioning, skin firming, redness reducer, scale reducer, and itch reducer.
Skin Deep Database Score: 1
Skin Deep Data Available: Limited
Source: Animal (organic) or plant (organic)

Panthenol (ProVitamin B5) is an anti-inflammatory and a redness reducer frequently used to improve damaged skin. DL-panthenol consists of half D-panthenol and half L-panthenol. The D-panthenol is easily absorbed by the skin and rapidly converted to pantothenic acid (vitamin B5), essential for cell health. The L-panthenol adds to product stability and is not converted to pantothenic acid but still offers the beneficial characteristic of being moisturizing. DL-panthenol is very hygroscopic and clumps together until dissolved in water. Dry white clumping powder. Add to water phase of products from 1% to 2% of the total weight of the product.

Dry panthenol (ProVitamin B5) powder.

PhytoCide
INCI: *Caprylic acid, propanediol, lauric acid, and potassium sorbate*
Purpose: Product broad spectrum preservative.
Skin Deep and information per ingredient:

	Caprylic acid	Propanediol	Lauric acid	Potassium sorbate
Database Scores	1	1	1	3
Data Available	Fair	Fair	Fair	Limited
Source	Plant (organic)	Plant (organic)	Plant (organic)	Plant (organic)

A truly natural preservative, although not water soluble, it is water miscible. Best in emulsions of oil and water (such as lotion, eye liner, or mascara), very thick serums, or water based products in conjunction with an emulsifier, such as polysorbate 20. PhytoCide may separate from thin water based products. Among all natural preservatives based on vegetable-derived ingredients, PhytoCide has one of the best standalone profiles with proven broad spectrum activity. Pale yellow fluid liquid. Add to water phase from 0.5% to 2% of the total weight of the product, which must have a final pH between 3.0 and 6.5. Extreme pH will damage this preservative.

Polysorbate 20 or **Polysorbate 80**
INCI: *Polysorbate 20 or polysorbate 80*
Purpose: Ingredient emulsifier, solubilizer, surfactant.
Skin Deep Database Score: 3
Skin Deep Data Available: Fair
Source: Plant (organic)

Polysorbate 20 or polysorbate 80, in the form of a yellow liquid, is a water-phase emulsifier. It will maintain the emulsification of essential oils and keep them blended into water based products. When adding essential or fragrance oils to a water-based serum, choose polysorbate 20 because it will effectively emulsify lighter oils into water with less thickening and less clouding than polysorbate 80. When adding base or carrier oils (such as grape seed oil or pumpkin seed oil) to a water-based serum, choose polysorbate 80 because it will effectively emulsify heavier oils into water but may also cause thickening and clouding. Measure out separately at 1.0% to 3.0% of the total weight of the product. Then, mix the measured polysorbate with the essential oil or fragrance oil before mixing the polysorbate/fragrance blend into the serum base.

Potassium Sorbate
INCI: *Potassium sorbate*
Synonyms: Sorbistat potassium.
Purpose: Product preservative only effective against mold and yeast.
Skin Deep Database Score: 3
Skin Deep Data Available: Limited
Source: Plant (organic)

Potassium sorbate is a natural cosmetic and food preservative. Potassium sorbate is very active against mold, fairly active against yeast, and ineffective against bacteria. It should only be used to supplement other preservatives in acidic products. Sold as "prills" or solid, white micro-noodles. To be effective, it must be used in cosmetic products that are pH 4.5 or lower and is most effective in products with a pH of 3.0. Potassium sorbate is very soluble in water; add to water phase. Use from 0.1 to 0.5%. Maximum use is 0.5%.

Propanediol
INCI: *Propanediol*
Synonyms: 1,3-propanediol.
Purpose: Skin humectant, conditioning, emollient.
Skin Deep Database Score: 1
Skin Deep Data Available: Fair
Source: Plant (organic)

A natural humectant, not petrochemical-sourced. Propanediol is very similar to glycerin but it is thinner and less viscous than glycerin, so it can be used in larger quantities without the sticky feel glycerin has in large amounts. Propanediol is a clear odorless humectant used to retain skin moisture. Acts as a solubilizer for small amounts of essential or fragrance oils, enabling them to mix into water. A clear viscous liquid. Add to water phase of products from 2% to 20% of the total weight of the product.

Silica

INCI: *Silica*
Synonyms: Hydrated silica, Silica dioxide hydrate, Silica hydrate, Silica gel, Silicon dioxide.
Purpose: Oil thickener, jellifying oil.
Skin Deep Database Score: 1
Skin Deep Data Available: Good
Source: Mineral (inorganic)

Silica is commonly added to dried herbs and seasonings to keep them free-flowing. It is also used in pill production. Silica absorbs oils to form a gel. Add to oil phase of mascara to create a thicker mascara and use less of the emulsifiers. Although cosmetic and food grades of silica are synthetic, silica does occur naturally in sand. Silica is a fine white powder that easily becomes airborne and is a respiratory irritant. Always wear a facemask when working with dry powdered silica. White dry powder. Add to oil phase of mascara recipe from 2% to 5% of the total weight of the product; allow up to 45 minutes for full hydration to occur; remember to decrease the emulsifiers or the mascara will be too thick.

Squalane

INCI: *Squalane*
Synonyms: Hydrogenated squalene, Olive squalane, Vegetable squalane, Vitabiosol.
Purpose: Skin humectant, conditioning, emollient.
Skin Deep Database Score: 1
Skin Deep Data Available: Limited
Source: Plant (organic)

Frequently called, "nature's facelift." Squalane is a botanical lipid that mirrors human lipids in molecular structure and weight. The skin's sebaceous glands synthesize 10-12% squalane. Squalane is not water soluble and requires the addition of an emulsifier, such as polysorbate 80. Clear viscous liquid. Add to the oil phase at 1% to 15% of the total weight of the product.

Stearic Acid

INCI: *Stearic acid*
Synonyms: Palm stearic, Palm stearin, Stearic fatty acid.
Purpose: Ingredient emulsifier, product thickener, skin conditioning.
Skin Deep Database Score: 1
Skin Deep Data Available: Fair
Source: Animal (organic) or plant (organic)

A natural emulsifier and thickener extracted from vegetable oil. Because it is a solid, it must be melted to be combined with other oil phase ingredients. Used in gel eyeliner and mascara as a natural thickener and to make products water resistant. White waxy flakes. Melts at 157° F. Add to oil phase of products from 2% to 20% of the total weight of the product.

Vitamin E
INCI: *Tocopherol*
Purpose: Skin conditioning, antioxidant.
Skin Deep Database Score: 1
Skin Deep Data Available: Fair
Source: Plant (organic)

A skin conditioning antioxidant that is very beneficial and nutritive to the skin. Prevents the oxidation of base oils and extends their shelf lives. Thick viscous amber liquid. Add to mascara oil phase at 0.5% to 1% of the total weight of the product. Cosmetic grade tocopherol is always dark brown to orange in color. Oral vitamin supplement capsules are not concentrated enough for cosmetics, as evident by the pale color. Tocopherol is never the main ingredient of "Vitamin E" supplement capsules, which frequently contain safflower, sunflower, and/or soybean oils as the main ingredient within the gelatin capsule. Seek concentrated, pure, cosmetic grade vitamin E.

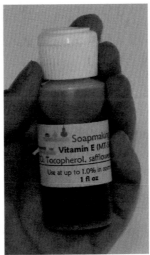

Cosmetic grade tocopherol is always dark brown to orange in color.

Chapter 5
Working with Serum Base

Serum base is a premade serum for sale to serum crafters. Although more expensive than hydroxyethyl cellulose powder, the serum base does away with the risk and wait involved in getting hydroxyethyl cellulose to full hydration. Prepared serum bases typically include some additoinal expensive and beneficial additives and are designed to save the crafter the labor time involved in working with the dry powdered HEC. It is simply a matter of choice: Does the crafter have the time and patience to hydrate the HEC powder and add substantial additives, or would the crafter benefit from a ready to use base? The average serum base is desigend to accommodate the addition of 20% more additives, possibly more if the ingredients are dry or powdered. The crafter must be careful to maintain the final product within the specific pH and temperature constraints of the preservative used in the serum base or be prepared to add additional preservative.

Dry aloe vera juice powder may be reconstituted with distilled water to make aloe vera juice.

For the serum base prepared in class, aloe vera juice powdered concentrate is re-constituted with distilled water to produce a slightly concentrated aloe vera juice. The serum base label should list these ingredients as "aloe vera juice." When working with the serum base, if adding more than 10% water to the serum base, the final product label must also list "water," unless more aloe vera powder is added.

After adding ingredients, always test the final pH of the product. The preservative system in the premade serum base requires a final pH below pH 6. If the pH is not clearly near 5.0, the pH must be adjusted. When working with serum base, to guarantee an acceptable pH, have both an Acidic pH Adjustment Solution (made from citric acid) and an Alkaline Adjustment Solution (made from sodium hydroxide) on hand, see page 21. If more than 20% additional ingredients are added, more preservative must be added. Furthermore, when adding customized ingredients, the serum base must not be heated above 176° F or the preservative system will be destroyed and more preservative should be added.

The serum base prepared in class is available as a prepared, ready to use serum base from SoapmakingStudio.com.

Chapter 6
pH Adjustment Solutions

Acidic pH Adjustment Solution (Citric Acid Solution)

Water Phase

Total Ounces to Make _5.00 oz_	Percentage (Must Total 100%)	Ingredient	Purpose
4.00 oz	80.00%	Distilled water	Solvent
1.00 oz	20.00%	Citric acid powder	Acidic to lower pH

Acidic pH Adjustment Solution: Prepare a 20% citric acid solution by dissolving 1 ounce of citric acid powder in 4 ounces of distilled water. Store the 20% citric acid solution in a separate container that is tightly sealed. The solution is acidic enough to prevent the growth of common microbes and does not require a preservative. This solution is used to make a product more acidic, less alkaline, or reduce the number on the pH scale.

0   7   14

Use the Acidic pH Adjustment Solution to lower the product pH.

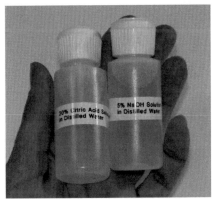

pH Adjustment Solutions

Alkaline pH Adjustment Solution (Sodium Hydroxide Solution)

Water Phase

Total Ounces to Make _5.00 oz_	Percentage (Must Total 100%)	Ingredient	Purpose
4.75 oz	95.00%	Distilled water	Solvent
0.25 oz	5.00%	Sodium hydroxide	Alkaline to raise pH

Alkaline pH Adjustment Solution: Prepare a 5% sodium hydroxide solution by dissolving 0.20 ounce of sodium hydroxide powder in 4.75 ounces of distilled water. Store the 5% sodium hydroxide solution in a separate container that is tightly sealed. The solution is alkaline enough to prevent the growth of common microbes and does not require a preservative. This solution is used to make a product less acidic, more alkaline, or increase the number on the pH scale.

0   7   14

Use the Alkaline pH Adjustment Solution to increase the product pH.

Chapter 7
Making Serum Base

Water Phase

Total Ounces to Make _30.00 oz_	Percentage (Must Total 100%)	Ingredient	Purpose
0.45 oz	1.50%	Hydroxyethyl cellulose	Gel base
0.15 oz	0.50%	Aloe vera juice powder	Skin conditioner
28.35 oz	94.50%	Distilled water	Gel base
0.60 oz	2.00%	Panthenol (ProVit B5)	Skin conditioner
0.45 oz	1.50%	Optiphen Plus	Preservative

For the main gel serum recipe: Dissolve aloe vera juice powder, panthenol, and Optiphen Plus preservative system in the recipe's 94.50% plain distilled water. Add hydroxyethyl cellulose and mix thoroughly for 20 minutes, include bursts of mechanical mixing from an immersion blender.

After 20 minutes of stirring, if some of the powder remains undissolved or if the hydroxyethyl cellulose is not hydrated and thick, slowly heat the mixture to 120° F.

> Trouble shooting:
> Take care not get the mixture too hot because the Optiphen Plus preservative system is denatured (destroyed) above 176° F. If the mixture is accidentally heated above 176° F, allow the mixture to cool and add another 1.50% Optiphen Plus.

Heat may increase the rate of hydration of the hydroxyethyl cellulose and cause it to thicken quickly, so continuous stirring and/or blending is required. Allow the mixture to cool while stirring. Full hydration may require 24 hours.

pH test tape provides more tests per dollar than pH test strips.

Test the pH of the final gel with pH test tape. The Optiphen Plus preservative requires the final product have a pH below 6.0. If the pH is not obviously between pH 4.0 and 6.0 when tested with pH tape, adjust the pH accordingly.

If the pH is above 6.0 it must be lowered to ensure preservative viability: To lower the pH add and mix in one drop at a time of the Acidic pH Adjustment Solution (citric acid solution), stir, and retest until a safe pH is achieved.

If the pH is below 4.0 it must be raised to ensure skin compatibility: To raise the pH add and mix in one drop at a time of the Alkaline pH Adjustment Solution (sodium hydroxide solution), stir, and retest until a safe pH is achieved.

Note: When working with the serum base, if adding more than 10% water to the serum base, the final product label must also list "water," unless more aloe vera powder is added. If more than 20% additional ingredients are added, more preservative will be needed.

When prepared to be used as a base for making other cosmetics, package the serum base into an a sterile or sanitary air-tight container, such as an empty distilled water jug. When packaging for sale to customers, use petite 1-ounce airless pumps to increase the shelf life of the water based serum. Airless pumps prevent the customer and air from contacting the product. One ounce of serum usually starts at about $35, due to the expense of the active ingredients.

Chapter 8
Aloe Vera Gel

This aloe vera gel is made from the premade serum base on page 23.

Water Phase

Total Ounces to Make __15.00 oz__	Percentage (Must Total 100%)	Ingredient	Purpose
13.20 oz	88.00%	Serum base (page 23)	Serum base
1.49 oz	9.99%	Distilled water	Solvent, thinner
0.30 oz	2.00%	Propanediol	Humectant, conditioner
0.01 oz	0.01%	Green food coloring	Colorant

Most consumers associate aloe vera gel with a green color. By mixing in a small amount of liquid green food coloring, additional distilled water, and propanediol, the serum is ready to be sold as a natural aloe vera gel.

For practical purposes, the distilled water could weigh 1.50 ounces and the 0.01 ounce of green food coloring could be added as one single drop.

Before packaging the aloe vera gel, remember to test the pH of the product. If the pH is not obviously between pH 4.0 and 5.0 when tested with pH tape, adjust the pH accordingly.

If the pH is near 6.0 it must be lowered to ensure preservative viability: To lower the pH add and mix in one drop at a time of the Acidic pH Adjustment Solution (citric acid solution), stir, and retest until a safe pH is achieved.

If the pH is below 4.0 it must be raised to ensure skin compatibility: To raise the pH add and mix in one drop at a time of the Alkaline pH Adjustment Solution (sodium hydroxide solution), stir, and retest until a safe pH is achieved.

This recipe makes a concentrated aloe vera gel, where a few drops of this serum contain as much aloe vera as several large squirts of a commercial gel. When packaging for sale to customers, use airless pumps to prevent the customer and air from contacting the product, include instructions to use only 2 or 3 drops (more may feel sticky or slimy), and include an ingredient declaration and other required labeling information.

Example of ingredient declaration for the aloe vera gel:
Ingredients: Aloe vera juice, propanediol, panthenol, hydroxyethyl cellulose, phenoxyethanol, caprylyl glycol, sorbic acid, glycerin, FD&C yellow #5, FD&C blue #1, citric acid, and sodium benzoate.

The "Phenoxyethanol, caprylyl glycol, and sorbic acid" are the ingredients from the preservative system with the trade name Optiphen Plus. The "glycerin, FD&C yellow #5, FD&C blue #1, citric acid, and sodium benzoate" are the ingredients from the 1 drop of green food coloring. If the pH was adjusted with a pH Adjustment Solution, remember to add either sodium hydroxide or citric acid to the ingredient declaration.

Chapter 9
Hand Sanitizers

Simple Hand Sanitizer

The simple hand sanitizer is made from the premade serum base on page 23.

Water Phase

Total Ounces to Make 10.00 oz	Percentage (Must Total 100%)	Ingredient	Purpose
7.00 oz	70.00%	Serum base (page 23)	Serum base
2.80 oz	28.00%	Isopropyl alcohol 91%	Antiseptic, sanitizer
0.20 oz	2.00%	Propanediol	Humectant, conditioner

For a quick and simple hand sanitizer, just mix all ingredients together with an immersion blender. The additives are greater than 20% and the isopropyl alcohol functions as an additional preservative. Remember, the final product must have a pH below 6.0 due to the constraints of the Optiphen Plus preservative system in the serum base. 28% alcohol may decrease the pH below 4.0 and a few drops of the Alkaline pH Adjustment Solution should be blended into the solution to achieve the goal of about pH 4.0 to pH 5.0.

Natural Hand Sanitizer

The natural hand sanitizer is made from scratch using hydroxyethyl cellulose and vodka.

Water Phase

Total Ounces to Make 10.00 oz	Percentage (Must Total 100%)	Ingredient	Purpose
0.40 oz	4.00%	Hydroxyethyl cellulose	Gel base
0.05 oz	0.50%	Aloe vera juice powder	Skin conditioner
9.20 oz	92.00%	Vodka (40%-80 proof)	Antiseptic, sanitizer
0.20 oz	2.00%	Panthenol (ProVit B5)	Skin conditioner
0.15 oz	1.50%	Optiphen Plus	Preservative

For a natural hand sanitizer, remake the serum base and use 40% alcohol (80 proof) vodka in the serum base. A natural, distilled alcohol with an ethanol content of 40% or more will kill most pathogenic bacterial. Follow the directions for serum base on page 23 but be sure to use the vodka instead of the distilled water, increase the hydroxyethyl cellulose to 4% and be prepared to adjust the pH with a pH Adjustment Solution to maintain a target pH between pH 4.0 and 5.0. The product pH must at least be below 6.0, as required by the Optiphen Plus preservative system.

Chapter 10
Skin Renewal Facial Serum

This serum is designed with active ingredients to promote cellular turnover. By helping to dissolve dead skin cells and reveal new, healthy cells, this serum effectively exfoliates to lighten skin, reduce redness, reduce dry flaky patches, and reduce acne.

Water Phase

Total Ounces to Make __10.00 oz__	Percentage (Must Total 100%)	Ingredient	Purpose
7.50 oz	75.00%	Serum base (page 23)	Serum base
1.50 oz	15.00%	Distilled water	Solvent, thinner
0.20 oz	2.00%	Allantoin	Skin healing, regeneration
0.50 oz	5.00%	Niacinamide (Vitamin B3)	Skin nutrient, lightener
0.20 oz	2.00%	Aspen bark extract	Beta hydroxy acid, preservative
0.10 oz	1.00%	Glycerin	Skin humectant, emollient

Add allantoin, niacinamide, and aspen bark extract powders to the distilled water. Mix by hand or immersion blender until powders are dissolved and mixture is clear. If the powdered additives are stubborn or slow to dissolve, the mixture may be heated to help them dissolve. Be careful not to heat the mixture above 140° F, which will denature with preservative qualities of the aspen bark extract. If the mixture is accidentally heated above 140° F, allow the mixture to cool and calculate the addition Optiphen Plus at the rate of 1% of the total weight of the product. Add the glycerin to the mixture and mix or blend it into the serum base. The additives are greater than 20% and the aspen bark extract functions as an additional preservative. No additional preservative is required if final product pH is below pH 6.0.

Before packaging the skin renewal facial serum, remember to test the pH of the product. If the pH is not obviously between pH 4.0 and 5.0 when tested with pH tape, adjust the pH accordingly.

If the pH is near 6.0 it must be lowered to ensure preservative viability: To lower the pH add and mix in one drop at a time of the Acidic pH Adjustment Solution (citric acid solution), stir, and retest until a safe pH is achieved.

If the pH is below 4.0 it must be raised to ensure skin compatibility: To raise the pH add and mix in one drop at a time of the Alkaline pH Adjustment Solution (sodium hydroxide solution), stir, and retest until a safe pH is achieved.

This recipe makes a concentrated skin renewal facial serum; one application consists of only a few drops. When packaging for sale to customers, use airless pumps to prevent the customer and air from contacting the product, include instructions to use only 2 or 3 drops (more may feel sticky or slimy), and include an ingredient declaration and other required labeling information.

Example of ingredient declaration for the skin renewal facial serum:
Ingredients: Aloe vera juice, niacinamide, water, allantoin, aspen bark extract, glycerin, panthenol, hydroxyethyl cellulose, phenoxyethanol, caprylyl glycol, and sorbic acid.

The "Phenoxyethanol, caprylyl glycol, and sorbic acid" are the ingredients from the preservative system with the trade name Optiphen Plus. If the pH was adjusted with a pH Adjustment Solution, remember to add either sodium hydroxide or citric acid to the ingredient declaration.

When packaging for sale to customers, use petite 1-ounce airless pumps to increase the shelf life of the water based serum. Airless pumps prevent the customer and air from contacting the product. One ounce of serum usually starts at about $35, due to the expense of the active ingredients.

Chapter 11
Concentrated Antioxidant Facial Serum

Concentrated Antioxidant Facial Serum

This serum contains extremely effective antioxidants to fight free radical damage, to improve the appearance of sun damaged skin, to help encourage collagen production for fuller and tighter looking skin, and to make mature skin look younger.

Water Phase

Total Ounces to Make _10.00 oz_	Percentage (Must Total 100%)	Ingredient	Purpose
7.00 oz	70.00%	Serum base (page 23)	Serum base
1.00 oz	10.00%	Distilled water	Solvent, thinner
0.20 oz	2.00%	Aspen bark extract	Beta hydroxy acid, preservative
0.80 oz	8.00%	Liposomal vitamin C	Antioxidant and nutrient
0.80 oz	8.00%	Liposomal CoQ10	Antioxidant and nutrient
0.20 oz	2.00%	Propanediol	Humectant, conditioner

Add aspen bark extract powder to the distilled water. Mix by hand or immersion blender until powder is dissolved and mixture is clear. Add the glycerin to the mixture. Heat the mixture to mixture to 140° F but not over 140° F because the aspen bark preservative will be destroyed over 140° F. Allow the mixture to cool below 110° F and mix in the liposomal vitamin C and liposomal CoQ10 by hand (do not use a mechanical mixer). Add the mixture to the serum base and mix by hand (do not use a mechanical mixer). Remember, liposomes may be damaged by mechanical mixing faster than 500 rpm or by heat above 110° F. The additives are greater than 20% and the aspen bark extract functions as an additional preservative. No additional preservative is required if final product pH is below pH 6.0.

Before packaging the concentrated antioxidant facial serum, remember to test the pH of the product. If the pH is not obviously between pH 4.0 and 5.0 when tested with pH tape, adjust the pH accordingly. Due to the high antioxidant content, this serum tends to be too acidic; if not adjusted, the acidic serum may be irritating to sensitive skin around the eye area and the user may experience a brief stinging sensation.

If the pH is near 6.0 it must be lowered to ensure preservative viability: To lower the pH add and mix in one drop at a time of the Acidic pH Adjustment Solution (citric acid solution), stir, and retest until a safe pH is achieved.

If the pH is below 4.0 it must be raised to ensure skin compatibility: To raise the pH add and mix in one drop at a time of the Alkaline pH Adjustment Solution (sodium hydroxide solution), stir, and retest until a safe pH is achieved.

This recipe makes a concentrated skin renewal facial serum; one application consists of only a few drops. When packaging for sale to customers, use airless pumps to prevent the customer and air from contacting the product, include instructions to use only 2 or 3 drops (more may feel sticky or slimy), and include an ingredient declaration and other required labeling information.

Example of ingredient declaration for the skin renewal facial serum:
Ingredients: Aloe vera juice, water, phospholipid, ubiquinone, glycerin, sodium ascorbyl phosphate, aspen bark extract, propanediol, panthenol, hydroxyethyl cellulose, phenoxyethanol, caprylyl glycol, sorbic acid, and sodium hydroxide.

The "water, phospholipid, ubiquinone, glycerin, and sodium ascorbyl phosphate" come from the liposomal C and liposomal CoQ10. The "Phenoxyethanol, caprylyl glycol, and sorbic acid" are the ingredients from the preservative system with the trade name Optiphen Plus. Most likely the pH was adjusted with the Alkaline pH Adjustment Solution to raise the pH, so remember to add the "sodium hydroxide" to the ingredient declaration.

When packaging for sale to customers, use petite 1-ounce airless pumps to increase the shelf life of the water based serum. Airless pumps prevent the customer and air from contacting the product. One ounce of serum usually starts at about $45, due to the expense of the active ingredients, especially the liposomes.

Many years ago, I sold a similar antioxidant facial serum for $30 per ounce but popularity and inflated ingredient prices have since driven the price up to $45 per ounce.

Chapter 12
Gel Eye Shadow

Gel Eye Shadow

Gel eye shadow is perfect for people with sensitive eyes. The addition of glycerin keeps this gel eye shadow lightly moist to keep the mica stuck to the eye lid and prevent it from flaking off into the eye.

Water Phase

Total Ounces to Make __10.00 oz__	Percentage (Must Total 100%)	Ingredient	Purpose
8.00 oz	80.00%	Serum base (page 23)	Serum base
0.70 oz	7.00%	Distilled water	Solvent, thinner
0.10 oz	1.00%	Glycerin	Skin humectant, emollient
1.20 oz	12.00%	Eye-safe mica	Colorant

Add eye-safe powdered mica to glycerin and smash with a flat spatula blade to disburse mica in glycerin. Add mica and glycerin to distilled water. Mix by hand or immersion blender until powder colorant is thoroughly wet and no lumps remain. Mix in the serum base. Pour the gel eye shadow into small, air tight pots. For squeeze tube packaging: If gel eye shadow is thin enough, pipe into squeeze tube with a pipette. If too thick for a pipette: Pour the gel eye shadow into the corner of a new (unused) plastic sandwich bag. Cut off a small corner to create a piping bag. To fill squeeze tubes, squeeze air from tube and release pressure to allow the tube to fill with gel eye shadow at the same time the gel is dispensed into the tube from the piping bag. Clean excess gel eye shadow from around top of tube. Screw on cap lightly. Apply with finger or dip a clean dry eye shadow brush into the gel and paint onto eyelid. Wash eye shadow brush with soap and water and dry brush. This recipe may easily be removed from the face with water. This recipe is considered hypoallergenic because it does not contain an emulsifier. If the gel eye shadow separates over time, simply shake the container to remix.

Note: Mica was recognized by the FDA in 1977 as being safe for use in "cosmetics generally, including the eye area." Do not use other additives for color around the eye area unless they have been approved for eye area use by the FDA.

Chapter 13
Gel Eyeliner

Gel Eyeliner

The glycerin in this gel eyeliner prevents the color from flaking off, which means less eye irritation. Best applied with a thin eyeliner brush, this gel eyeliner is actually made as a lotion and is very similar in formulation to the mascara. The stearic acid and cetearyl alcohol serve as emulsifiers, while the cyclomethicone is very emollient and allows the product to be spread easily and evenly. Cyclomethicone is also beneficial because it evaporates quickly, which gives the gel eyeliner a quick drying time.

Water Phase

Total Ounces to Make __10.00 oz__	Percentage (Must Total 100%)	Ingredient	Purpose
6.50 oz	65.00%	Serum base (page 23)	Serum base
0.50 oz	5.00%	Distilled water	Solvent, thinner
0.10 oz	1.00%	Glycerin	Skin humectant, emollient
1.00 oz	10.00%	Eye-safe powder*	Colorant
0.05 oz	0.50%	PhytoCide	Preservative

*FDA approved colorants for eye area use include black iron oxide, brown iron oxide, ultramarine (blue) and green chromium oxide, which are all available as powdered mineral pigments. Do not use unapproved colorants (such as activated charcoal) near the eye area. For a list of cosmetic colorants approved by the FDA for eye area use, visit http://www .fda.gov/ForIndustry/ColorAdditives/ColorAdditiveInventories/ucm115641.htm#table3A

Oil Phase

0.40 oz	4.00%	Stearic acid	Emulsifier, thickener
0.40 oz	4.00%	Cetearyl alcohol 30/70	Emulsifier, thickener
0.05 oz	0.50%	Vitamin E	Skin conditioning, antioxidant
1.00 oz	10.00%	Cyclomethicone	Lash conditioning, emollient

Add eye-safe powdered colorant, glycerin, and PhytoCide preservative to the distilled water. Mix by hand or immersion blender until powder colorant is thoroughly wet and no lumps remain. Mix in the serum base. Heat the water phase mixture to mixture to 130° F. Combine and heat the stearic acid and cetearyl alcohol until completely melted, about 155° F. To the melted stearic acid and cetearyl alcohol, add the cyclomethicone and vitamin E, which will cool the mixture a bit. Mix and maintain the temperature of the oil phase combination of ingredients at about 130° F or just warm enough to keep the oil phase ingredients melted. Add warm water phase mixture to warm oil phase mixture and mix with a mechanical mixer. Continue blending as the mixture cools. No additional preservative is required if final product pH is between pH 3.0 and pH 6.0. For the sensitive eye area, if the pH is not obviously near 5.0 when tested with pH tape, adjust the pH with one drop at a time of pH Adjustment Solution and retest until a safe pH is achieved. While gel eyeliner is still warm, pour into small, air tight pots.

To apply the gel eyeliner, dip a clean dry eyeliner brush into the gel and paint onto eyelid at base of eyelashes. Wash eyeliner brush with soap and water and dry brush. This recipe may easily be removed from the face with soap and water; it is water resistant and smudge resistant after it has dried on the skin. To create a waterproof formula, add 5% bees wax to the oil phase ingredients and decrease the serum base to 60%, so the total of all percentages will still total 100%.

Chapter 14
Mascara

The glycerin in this mascara prevents the color from flaking off, which means less eye irritation. This mascara is actually made as a lotion and is very similar in formulation to the gel eyeliner. The stearic acid and cetearyl alcohol serve as emulsifiers, while the cyclomethicone is very emollient and allows the lashes to easily be separated when brushed. Cyclomethicone is also beneficial because it evaporates quickly, which gives the mascara a quick drying time.

Water Phase

Total Ounces to Make _10.00 oz_	Percentage (Must Total 100%)	Ingredient	Purpose
6.00 oz	60.00%	Serum base (page 23)	Serum base
0.50 oz	5.00%	Distilled water	Solvent, thinner
0.10 oz	1.00%	Glycerin	Skin humectant, emollient
1.50 oz	15.00%	Eye-safe powder*	Colorant
0.05 oz	0.50%	PhytoCide	Preservative

*FDA approved colorants for eye area use include black iron oxide, brown iron oxide, ultramarine (blue) and green chromium oxide, which are all available as powdered mineral pigments. Do not use unapproved colorants (such as activated charcoal) near the eye area. For a list of cosmetic colorants approved by the FDA for eye area use, visit http://www .fda.gov/ForIndustry/ColorAdditives/ColorAdditiveInventories/ucm115641.htm#table3A

Oil Phase

0.40 oz	4.00%	Stearic acid	Emulsifier, thickener
0.40 oz	4.00%	Cetearyl alcohol 30/70	Emulsifier, thickener
0.05 oz	0.50%	Vitamin E	Skin conditioning, antioxidant
1.00 oz	10.00%	Cyclomethicone	Lash conditioning, emollient

Add eye-safe powdered colorant, glycerin, and PhytoCide preservative to the distilled water. Mix by hand or immersion blender until powder colorant is thoroughly wet and no lumps remain. Mix in the serum base. Heat the water phase mixture to mixture to 130° F. Combine and heat the stearic acid and cetearyl alcohol until completely melted, about 155° F. To the melted stearic acid and cetearyl alcohol, add the cyclomethicone and vitamin E, which will cool the mixture a bit. Mix and maintain the temperature of the oil phase combination of ingredients at about 130° F or just warm enough to keep the oil phase ingredients melted. Add warm water phase mixture to warm oil phase mixture and mix with a mechanical mixer. Continue blending as the mixture cools. No additional preservative is required if final product pH is between pH 3.0 and pH 6.0. For the sensitive eye area, if the pH is not obviously near 5.0 when tested with pH tape, adjust the pH with one drop at a time of pH Adjustment Solution and retest until a safe pH is achieved.

While mascara is still warm, pour into the corner of an unused plastic sandwich bag. Cut off a small corner to create a piping bag. To fill mascara tubes, squeeze air out of the mascara tube and release pressure to allow the tube to fill with mascara at the same time the mascara is dispensed into the tube from the piping bag. Clean excess mascara from around top of tube. Insert wiper into tube top. (The wiper ring insert creates a smaller opening so excess mascara is removed or "wiped off" of the brush as it is removed from the tube.) Insert brush into tube through wiper and tighten cap.

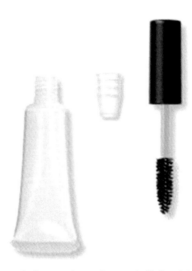

Mascara tube, wiper insert, lid with brush.

To apply, brush mascara onto eyelashes with a clean sweeping motion. Do not apply mascara to top side of upper lashes. This recipe may easily be removed from the lashes with soap and water; it is water resistant and smudge resistant after it has dried on the lashes. To create a waterproof formula, add 5% bees wax to the oil phase ingredients and decrease the serum base to 55%%, so the total of all percentages will still total 100%.

Notes

Notes

Notes

Notes

Notes

Bookstore

The Soapmaking Studio Bookstore is available online by clicking "Bookstore" from www.SoapmakingStudio.com or by visiting the bookstore directly: http://astore.amazon.com/soapstudio-20

Refer to this list of Bookstore categories because the Amazon format will not allow all possible category options to be viewed at the same time. Orders are fulfilled by Amazon.

Soapmaking Studio Bookstore

- Soapmaking
    - Cold Process
        - Beginning
        - Intermediate
            - Milk Soap
        - Advanced
    - Hot Process
        - Liquid Soap
        - Transparent Bar Soap
        - Opaque Bar Soap
    - Melt and Pour
    - Rebatching

- Cosmetics

- New Books

- Magazines

- Business
    - Start a Soap Business
    - Labeling and Packaging
    - Accounting
    - Business Entities

- Chemistry

- Fiction

- Gardening

- Miscellaneous
    - Appliances and Electronics
    - Essential Oils
    - Kindle Books
    - Unavailable

- Libros en Español

Soapmaking Studio
Registration Form

Student's Name: _____

Mailing Address: _____

City, State ZIP: _____

Telephone: _____

Email: _____

Registration for enrollment in the following class:

☐ Soapmaking 101, Beginning Cold Process Soapmaking

☐ Soapmaking 105, Intermediate Hot Process Soapmaking

☐ Soapmaking 210, Advanced Cold/Hot Process Soapmaking

☐ Soapmaking 214, Intermediate Transparent Bar Soapmaking

☐ Soapmaking 215, Intermediate Liquid Soapmaking

☐ Soapmaking 220, Coloring and Scenting Soap

☐ Soap Garden 224, Cultivating, Drying, and Adding Herbs to Soap

☐ Soapmaking 225, Water Substitution in Soapmaking

☐ Soap Business 320, Forming a Legal Business Entity to Sell Soap

☐ Soap Business 330, Soap Labeling and Marketing

☐ Soap Business 335, Shrink Wrapping Soap

☐ Soap Business 340, Packaging and Shipping Soap Worldwide

☐ Soap Business 350, Website Design and Internet Commerce

☐ Cosmetic Making Class: _____

Class information:

Class Date: _____

Class Time: _____

Instructor: _____

Class Fee: _____

Materials Fee: _____

Total Enrollment Fee: _____

Make check or money order payable to the Soapmaking Studio and mail to:

Soapmaking Studio
7301 Mount Vernon St
Lemon Grove, CA 91945-3122

Before mailing, make a copy of your completed registration form for your records.
Contact the Soapmaking Studio with any questions: (619) 668-1435 • info@SoapmakingStudio.com

39942171R00036

Made in the USA
Middletown, DE
29 January 2017